Feb. 12 week.

En Pièces Détachées

a play by Michel Tremblay

translated by Allan Van Meer

Vancouver Talonbooks 1975

published with assistance from the Canada Council

Talonbooks
201 1019 East Cordova
Vancouver
British Columbia V6A 1M8
Canada

This book was typeset by Linda Gilbert of B.C. Monthly
Typesetting Service, and designed by David Robinson.

First printing: September 1975

Talonplays are edited by Peter Hay.

Rights to produce *En Pièces Détachées,* in whole or in part,
in any medium by any group, amateur or professional, are
retained by the author, and interested persons are requested
to apply to his agent, John Goodwin, 3823 Melrose Avenue,
Montreal, Quebec H4A 2S3, who is authorized to negotiate.

This script is a translation of the television version of the play.

First published by Les Editions Leméac Inc., Montréal, Québec.
Published by arrangement with Les Editions Leméac Inc.

ISBN 0-88922-092-1

En Pièces Détachées was first performed at Théâtre de Quat'
Sous in Montréal, Québec, on April 23, 1969, with the following cast:

The Neighbours	Monique Joly
Robertine and Mado	Hélène Loiselle
Hélène	Luce Guilbault
Francine and Lise	Christine Olivier
Henri	Jean Archambault
Claude	Claude Gai

Directed by André Brassard
Designed by Germain

En Pièces Détachées was first performed on French language CBC-TV in the series, "Beaux Dimanches," on March 6, 1971. It was re-broadcast on July 23, 1972. The cast was as follows:

Thérèse	Luce Guilbault
Robertine	Hélène Loiselle
Marcel	Claude Gai
Joanne	Christine Olivier
Gérard	Roger Garand
Lucille	Monique Miller
Mado	Sophie Clément
Lise	Micheline Pomranski
Toothpick	Jean Archambault
M.C.	Jacques Bilodeau
The Aurora Sisters	Odette Gagnon, Nicole LeBlanc, Monique Rioux
Paul	Ernest Guimond
Maurice	Jean Duceppe
Dishwasher	Normand Morin
The Neighbours	Monique Joly, Micheline Gérin, Colette Devlin, Suzanne Langlois, Germaine Giroux, Rita Lafontaine, Sylvie Heppel, Yolande Roy, Colette Courtois.

Directed by Paul Blouin
Set Design by Gabriel Perreault
Costumes by Claudette Picard

En Pièces Détachées was first performed in English as "Like Death Warmed Over" at the Manitoba Theatre Centre in Winnipeg, Manitoba, on January 17, 1973, with the following cast:

Hélène	Dana Ivey
Robertine	Irene Hogan
Claude	Heath Lamberts
Francine and Lise	Margaret Bard
Henri and Toothpick	Michael Donaghue
Mado and Lucille	Liza Creighton

Directed by André Brassard
Designed by Real Ouellette
Lighting Designed by Kent McKay

En Pièces Détachées was also performed in English as "Broken Pieces" at the Arts Club Theatre in Vancouver, British Columbia, on October 10, 1974, with the following cast:

Hélène	Lally Cadeau
Robertine	Doris Chillcott
Claude	David Stein
Francine and Lise	Fiona Law
Henri	David Major
Mado and Lucille	Anna-May McKellar

Directed by Bill Millerd
Designed by Charles Van Vliet
Lighting Designed by Marsha Sibthorpe

one

The courtyard of a tenement block, somewhere in the East End of Montréal. It is summer. Very hot. The women are out getting some fresh air after supper, some set up at their windows with pillows or cushions, bottles of pop, potato chips, radios; others (those that have them) sitting on their balconies or on the fire escape that runs in front of their windows.

Long silence before the first line (long enough to feel how wilted and sluggish the women are), then, as soon as MME. TREMBLAY has spoken, the courtyard comes to life . . .

The lines of this first scene may blend together, crisscrossing, leapfrogging . . .

MME. TREMBLAY:
Michel . . . Michel, bring in your bike now, it's getting dark!

MME. BELANGER:
That coke didn't last long!

MME. TREMBLAY:
Michel!

MME. BELANGER:
Aurèle, get me another coke, wouldya?!

MME. TREMBLAY:
Michel, don't you go running off, you hear me?

MME: MENARD:
André, sweetheart, you come up here on the porch now.

MME. BELANGER:
Aurèle, whatsa matter, are you deaf?

MME. MENARD:
Come on dear, I've told you, you're not supposed to play with Monique Beaulieu . . .

MME. BEAULIEU:
Well, well, now! And just what's the matter with my Monique, eh?! She hasn't got the mange, for heaven's sake!

MME. TREMBLAY:
Michel! You're gonna get a good smack across the face if you don't answer me!

MME. MENARD:
I just don't like the boys playing with the girls down in the yard after dark, that's all.

MME. BELANGER:
And don't go bringing me a warm one, either! I want a cold one!

MME. BEAULIEU:
Well, what harm isat gonna do them? . . . They're too young for that sorta thing, surely . . .

MME. TREMBLAY:
Michel!

MME. MONETTE:
Ah, quit your hollerin' over there, Jesus! He's already gone, that Michel of yours! He took off with his bike. He's not gonna hear you all the way from Papineau Street!

MME. MENARD:
Not as young as you think, Mme. Beaulieu, mark my words! It's best to keep an eye on them, just in case!

MME. BELANGER:
Just like I figured, a warm one!

MME. SOUCY:
Michel! Michel! I just saw him go by, Mme. Tremblay!

MMES. TREMBLAY & SOUCY:
Michel! Michel!

MME. MONETTE:
That's it, the both of you go at it now! The police'll be down here for sure!

MME. BELANGER: *to her husband*
You still haven't put up that clothes line yet! Everybody's done their wash except me! Well, I'm gonna end up having to do it one way or another! I don't care, that's fine with me, only I'm gonna have to hang it in the house again!

MME. SOUCY:
I'll watch out for him, Mme. Tremblay. If I see him, I'll let you know.

MME. MONETTE:

> You old tattle-tale, you! Why don't you let that
> child play once in a while? He's always hanging from
> his mother's apron strings. You know what you'll
> end up turning your son into, Mme. Tremblay?

MME. TREMBLAY:

> Better that than he should grow up a bum, like that
> Richard of yours, Mme. Monette!

MME. BELANGER:

> And then you'll be grumbling again about the whole
> house being damp!

MME. BERNIER: *to MME. BEAULIEU*

> And what's more, he told me I was on the verge of
> anemia.

MME. BEAULIEU:

> Oh yes, I've had that too, that's no fun, that stuff,
> but I'm pretty well over it now.

MME. MONETTE:

> Hey, Mme. Soucy, Mme. Tremblay's Michel just went
> by . . . didn't you holler at him?

MME. SOUCY:

> Michel! Michel!

MME. TREMBLAY:

> Did you see him, the little rascal. Michel, you little
> son-of-a-gun, I'm gonna break your leg for you, and
> then see how far you can pedal!

MME. BELANGER:

> Ah, shut up, Armand, for Chrissake! If I wanna
> drink a whole case of cokes for once in a blue moon,
> it's my own damn business.

MME. BEAULIEU:

What you need is iron, Mme. Bernier. Get yourself
some iron vitamins!

MME. BERNIER:

Vitamins! Vitamins! They cost money, those
vitamins!

MME. BEAULIEU:

If you want, I think I've still got a bottle left over
here . . .

MME. SOUCY:

Hey, be careful, Mme. Bernier! Vitamins are different
for everybody . . . It's never a good idea taking some-
body else's vitamins . . .

MME. BEAULIEU:

Oh come on, it was my sister-in-law gave me these . . .

MME. SOUCY:

And you don't look so all-fired healthy yourself . . .

MME. BEAULIEU:

Monique! Monique! I think maybe you were right,
Mme. Menard, you know that? . . . What are those
kids doing down there, anyway?! . . .

MME. SOUCY:
Michel!

MME. TREMBLAY:

Michel! You're gonna get the spanking stick is what
you're gonna get!

MME. MENARD:
André!

MME. BEAULIEU:
Monique!

To MME. BERNIER

Have you known for very long . . . About the other
thing, I mean?

MME. BERNIER:
No, I just found out yesterday . . . The roof is gonna
come down in our place when that gets out, let me
tell you. I've already got three . . .

MME. SOUCY:
Yeah . . . Well, yeah . . . And you're so young . . .
You won't be able to stay in that four room place
of yours though . . . You'll have to move . . .

MME. MENARD:
André!

MME. BEAULIEU:
Monique!

MME. BERNIER:
Move? My old man has trouble movin' his ass from
one armchair to another. The heartless bastard!

MME. MENARD:
I think we're going to have to go down there, this
is ridiculous . . .

MME. MONETTE:
No, no, they're not under the porch anymore. I just
saw them go out of the yard . . . Boy, can they get on
a person's nerves!

MME. BEAULIEU:
Your André already running off with the girls, Mme.
Menard? Takes right after his father, eh? . . .

14

MMES. TREMBLAY,
SOUCY & MONETTE:
    Michel! Michel!

MME. TREMBLAY: *to MME. MONETTE*
    So you're yelling with us now, all of a sudden?

MME. MONETTE:
    The police'll be here even sooner!

MME. MENARD:
    So what is it about his father that you find so
    interesting, Mme. Beaulieu?

MME. BEAULIEU:
    Oh, he doesn't interest me, not me . . . Not at all . . .
    But of course, there's others . . .

MME. MENARD:
    Who? Name 'em, who?

MME. BERNIER: *who has heard them*
    Well, I think I'd just as well go in now . . .

MME. BEAULIEU: *knowing smile*
    I wasn't only thinking of you, Mme. Bernier . . .

MME. SOUCY:
    Michel! Michel! I just saw him go by, Mme. Tremblay,
    I just saw him go by!

MME. TREMBLAY:
    Ah, well, never mind now . . . No sense yellin' yourself
    hoarse for nothing . . . I just hope he has an accident,
    that's all!

ALL THE WOMEN:
    Honestly, Mme. Tremblay, you're about as heartless
    as they come!

*All of a sudden we see ROBERTINE slowly
closing her venetian blinds.*

*All the heads turn automatically towards
ROBERTINE's window.*

*MME. L'HEUREUX and MME. GINGRAS
appear for the first time. They are both leaning
out of neighbouring windows, elbows on the
sills. It is as if they had just "surfaced." They
never speak to each other or look at each other.*

MME. L'HEUREUX:
> She just shut the blinds . . . Joseph, the nut across the
> yard just went an' shut her venetian blinds again . . .

MME. GINGRAS:
> Gettin' all set for another battle royal, sure as any-
> thing . . .

> *The women all shift themselves so as to get
> a better view.*

> *An unhealthy curiosity is legible on each face.*

ALL THE WOMEN: *very slowly*
> Gettin' all set for another battle royal, sure as
> anything . . .

> *MME. L'HEUREUX leans forward a bit.*

MME. L'HEUREUX:
> No! Well, I'll be . . . Joseph, guess what! Henri just
> opened the blinds again! Believe it or not, Henri just
> up and opened the blinds!

MME. GINGRAS:
>That's the first time in his life that man has ever stood
>up to his mother-in-law . . . Must have a bit of gumption
>left in him after all, I guess . . . Here, an' I figured he
>had about as much backbone as a bowlful o' Jello!

>*The women laugh.*

MME. L'HEUREUX:
>Well, holy bells of Christmas . . .

ALL THE WOMEN:
>She just closed 'em again!

MME. L'HEURFUX:
>She shut them blinds right on his nose.

MME. GINGRAS:
>They keep this up all night, those blinds'll be crashin'
>down on their heads before they know it.

>*Pause.*

>*The women, craning their necks, await further
>action.*

MME. L'HEUREUX:
>Just like I figured . . . They'll be stayin' shut now . . .

ALL THE WOMEN:
>Gettin' all set for another battle royal, if you ask me . . .

MME. GINGRAS:
>Henri's said his last say. Now he'll just clam up and
>take it all in, as usual . . .

MME. MONETTE:
>The wife and her old lady yappin' in his ears all night,
>and he won't say a word. Goddam fool!

MME. TREMBLAY:
> Boy, I'd be long gone outa that hen house if I was in
> his shoes! 'Course, there's nothing much he can do
> about it, that's true . . . Doesn't even go out of the
> house any more . . . Before his accident though . . .

MME. BEAULIEU:
> Now that accident, that's another thing. Nobody
> actually saw that, did they? . . .

MME. L'HEUREUX:
> Before his accident, he was a real non-stop griper,
> that Henri was. Get up gripin' in the mornin', go to
> bed gripin' at night . . . These days though, not a peep
> out of him . . . Not a word. Drinks his beer . . .
> Watches TV . . . That's it . . . Just resigned himself
> to it all, I suppose . . .

MME. GINGRAS:
> Poor Henri.

MME. L'HEUREUX:
> Well, there's no reason I should go feelin' sorry for
> him, I guess. The last thing anybody in that goddam
> house needs is somebody feeling sorry for them.

MMES. L'HEUREUX
& GINGRAS:
> Nothin' they like better than wallowing in their own
> misery!

MME. GINGRAS:
> They live in it up to their ears, and they'll die in it!
> Drown in it!

MME. L'HEUREUX:
> Joseph . . . Joseph, how long ago was it now Henri
> had his accident? That's right, don't answer me! Just

sit glued to that damn TV set and don't bother about
me! Honestly Joseph, you're such a bump on a log
the only bit of excitement I get out of life is sitting
here gawking at the neighbours.

MME. MENARD:
Well, one day here a while back, he came home with
a limp . . . Said he'd fallen off a ladder . . . Sat himself
down in his armchair and hasn't budged since.

MME. TREMBLAY:
He was such a good lookin' man though . . .

MME. L'HEUREUX:
When he and Hélène first started going steady . . .

MME. GINGRAS: *rolling her eyes*
"Going steady," well, that's one way of putting it,
I suppose . . .

MME. L'HEUREUX:
Hell, that must be goin' on twenty years ago now . . .
When he and Hélène first started going steady, every
girl on the block was just crazy about him . . . We'd
all come out on our balconies at night just to watch
him and Hélène going out together . . .

MME. SOUCY:
And Hélène, was she ever some doll, let me tell you.
And such a character she was, too.

MME. MONETTE:
Treated her folks just like dirt. Always had to have
her own way, that one . . .

MME. BEAULIEU:
Couldn't reason with her!

MMES. MONETTE,
SIMARD & MENARD:
Stubborn as a mule!

19

MME. L'HEUREUX:
>   And when the word got out she was gettin' married,
>   and to handsome Henri yet, well, the whole
>   neighbourhood was just on pins and needles.

MME. MONETTE:
>   Especially with it coming so sudden, and all!

>   *The women begin to laugh peculiarly. Their*
>   *laughing gets louder and louder until HELENE*
>   *shouts "Ok, maybe I ain't . . ."*

MME. L'HEUREUX:
>   The morning of the wedding the whole block was
>   out on the sidewalk waiting to see her come out.

MME. GINGRAS:
>   After all, she was the best lookin' girl in the
>   neighbourhood . . .

MME. L'HEUREUX:
>   Well as soon as she stepped out of that door, everybody
>   knew right away.

MME. BEAULIEU:
>   That's one bride wasn't wearing any lily white gown . . .

MME. MENARD:
>   No sir! Far from it . . .

MME. BELANGER:
>   She had on . . . a velveteen strapless . . .

ALL THE WOMEN:
>   In midnight blue !

MME. GINGRAS:
>Well, we didn't need any crystal ball to figure out
>what that meant . . . She walked down those steps
>through all that hooting and catcalling . . . Just before
>she got into the rent-a-car, she looked back at us all
>and hollered out:

>*Hélène's wedding sequence.*

>*HELENE appears in her wedding dress.*
>*She yells.*

HELENE:
>Ok, so maybe I ain't dressed in white, but I got him,
>didn't I?!

>*Long silence.*

>*The women seem hypnotised.*

MME. L'HEUREUX:
>I can still see her to this day, standing there with her
>red hair . . . She'd had it dyed the day before the
>wedding, but the hairdresser botched up the permanent
>and her hair came out fire engine red! What a sight,
>it was just too much for words, the bride in her mid-
>night blue dress and that flaming red hair!

MME. TREMBLAY:
>She didn't look like any cupid, let me tell you, she
>looked like the devil himself!

MME. MONETTE:
>And the rest of us on the sidewalk, we didn't think
>twice about tellin' her so, either!

ALL THE WOMEN: *on various tones*
>Devil Woman! Hey, Devil Woman!

HELENE appears again in her wedding dress,
a tragic look on her face, as if she were a
hundred years old.

MMES. L'HEUREUX
& GINGRAS:
Maybe she did get her man, but she's sure paid for it!

ALL THE WOMEN:
Oh yes, she's paid for it alright!

MME. MENARD:
Thanks to him she's been living on pork 'n beans
since the honeymoon. And now . . .

MME. TREMBLAY:
Now she's working over at Nick's, on Papineau Street!

MME. MONETTE:
She got herself fired from the club she was working
in for drinking on the job too often, and they scratched
her from their waitress list.

MME. L'HEUREUX:
She'll end up in some dive, and that's about all she's
good for!

MME. GINGRAS:
She'll end up in some dive, and that's about all she's
good for!

ALL THE WOMEN:
She'll end up in some dive, and that's about all she's
good for!

Music.

During the music the women can be heard
yelling, singing, screaming: "She'll end up
in some dive, and that's about all she's good
for!"

two

*Nick's Restaurant. A place selling smoked meat
sandwiches (among other things). The three
waitresses are not seen right away.*

*The cart into which the waitresses put the dirty
dishes might be seen, or even the dishwasher's
sink, but* no *full plates or appetizing dishes.*

*We hear HELENE and LISE hollering orders,
HELENE in a loud, authoritative, confident
voice; LISE in a weak, somewhat hesitant, timid
voice.*

HELENE:

One double submarine all dressed, one grill cheese,
two cold slaw, two coffees!

LISE:

One today's special, with no peas, and . . . Uh . . .
A coke . . . No, a seven-up . . . No, that's right, a coke,
pardon me!

HELENE:

>One pizza all dressed, medium, no cheese, one pastrami sand with pickles, one goulash, one wiener an' beans, four coffees . . .

LISE:

>Do you have canned corn?

HELENE:

>This is no time to be askin' 'em for canned corn! Don't you think they're busy enough as it is?

LISE:

>Well, anyway, a toasted cheese sandwich, with no canned corn.

HELENE:

>One fish 'n chips, one shepherd's pie, one western omelette, one chicken fried rice, six egg rolls, two ginger ales, one coffee . . . One tea.

>>*We see the three employees of Nick's place during the slack hour of the afternoon. All three are seated at the same booth. HELENE and LISE fold paper napkins while MADO, the cashier and girlfriend of the boss, manicures her nails. A lovely, brown, coagulated blood coloured nail polish would be perfect.*

HELENE:

>Hey, I'm tellin' ya, did I ever give him an earful! Think you can get smart with me, do ya, I says to him, think you can push me around and get away with it?! Well, just watch your step, buster! I've taken on tougher customers than you, a lot tougher!

MADO:

>You sure told 'im alright, Hélène!

HELENE: *to LISE*

> You should have seen him, he turned beet red right
> there. Mado here was just about splittin' herself
> over at the fountain. Couldn't keep a straight face
> if she tried!

MADO:

> I know, I know! You're such a scream, Hélène!
> It's worth a million just to watch you in action!

LISE:

> I just don't know how you do it, talking back to
> them the way you do, Hélène! You've just got so
> much crust!

HELENE:

> Listen, I worked long enough over on St. Lawrence,
> and I don't scare easy. I've seen plenty, believe you
> me. Slobbering drunks crawling on their knees, the
> whole bit. Done my share of bouncing too. And
> whoever thinks I'm gonna take any lip from some
> little punk on Papineau Street, they better think
> twice.

MADO:

> And besides, you had every right to say what you
> did! You hadn't been rude or anything! I saw it all,
> and if anybody asks me, I say good for you, you did
> just the right thing.

HELENE:

> Well, hell, that's just it. I wouldn't be saying this if
> I'd been buggin' him or something. I just didn't
> understand what he was ordering, that's all. You
> know how it is, it happens sometimes . . . You can't
> make out what the customer's asking for, especially
> when it's crowded. And on top of it all this guy was
> one of those Frenchmen . . . You know, those pissy
> little two-bit Frenchmen. Haven't got two nickels
> to rub together, but they're French up to here, and
> they won't let you forget it. This one, you couldn't

make out half of what he was saying, his mouth was
movin' like a turkey's ass. It ain't Paris here, that's all
I can say. Now, myself, I know I'm just the waitress,
ok, so I ask him as polite as anything to repeat himself.
I says to him in my best French, "Could you repeat
that again, please, I didn't understand." So then
he looks down his nose at me like I'm a can of
worms and says, "Are you deaf, or what? . . ." You
know how they talk. 'I asked you for a cup of tea,
mademoiselle. A cup of tea. T. E. A. Tea!" Just like
that. Well, about now I'm really startin' to see red,
right?! "Look here, shorty," I says to him, "you're
not coming in here to tell me how to spell tea, ok?
Look at me. Take a good look, over this way, buster!
I've got just as much schooling as you got over there
in France, maybe more, and I'm not here to stand and
have the likes o' you spelling tea at me in my face, ok?"

LISE:

I don't know how you do it, Hélène! I just can't
answer back to them the way you do. I just can't.
I get all nervous when they talk to me like that.

HELENE:

Well, you're not thick skinned enough with the
customers. You let 'em walk all over you.

LISE:

Yes, but Hélène, don't you think that's going a bit
too far? I mean, St. Lawrence and Papineau Street
are two different things. You can't talk to them
around here the way you can over there!

HELENE:

No, no, I know what you mean, but listen a minute,
Lise . . . When you're busy and you've been hustling
from one end of the joint to the other for two hours
and you've got twenty-five customers to wait on, you

know as well as I do, you're ready to drop. Good Lord, you're in no mood to stand gabbing with some little punks that take up a booth for a whole hour to eat a side of fries and then buzz off without leaving a plug nickel on the table!

LISE:

Yes, but you have to put up with those guys just the same. They're customers, just like everybody else.

HELENE:

Not when you're busy, not on your life! Ask any waitress you like. Not in your rush hours. Come on, you'd have to be outa your mind! When they come in in the middle of the afternoon then I don't care, I put up with them, but just don't let anybody rub me the wrong way during meal hours. You shouldn't put up with them, you shouldn't, that's all. And you complain that you're not makin' as much money as me! Well, I don't doubt it! You're just too nice with people! Ask Mado . . . Mado, when you were workin' the floor, you couldn'a let them push you around the way she does? . . .

MADO:

Me? Heh, I was the terror of Papineau Street!

LISE laughs.

It's the truth! You think Hélène is tough, Lise? You shoulda seen me on the floor! Let me tell you, there was nobody, I mean *no*body, tried to get smart with me! I have seen days, honey, without a word of a lie, I have seen days when I'd do that whole floor myself because the other girl was sick, and not make one single mistake! How does that grab you? Nobody stepped on my toes, or they soon found out who was boss in a hurry! You wanna smoked meat, baby?

Well don't change your mind now, mama ain't got
time . . . That's how you have to talk to 'em! Other-
wise the first thing you know, they're after you like
a pack o' hornets, orderin' this, orderin' that, till you
can't hear yourself think anymore and you're right
off your nut!

LISE:

Yes, but you, you've all got experience . . . This is
just my first job . . .

MADO:

Yeah, well, don't worry . . . It'll all sink in in time . . .

HELENE:

Just a minute now, I'm not so sure about that! Either
you have it, or you don't, I say! Take me now, I
started out down at Kresge's beside Eaton's there,
didn't know a damn word of English, and I held my
own . . . They'd be askin' me for cheese sandwiches
in English and I'd be bringin' 'em ham sandwiches
in French! And I'd holler so loud if they complained,
they'd end up eatin' their ham sandwiches and likin'
it . . . And in French too!

MADO: *by now getting rather irritated by Hélène*
Listen, when I started out, I was just as dumb as Lise
here, and I made my way just the same!

LISE:

I'm not that dumb! It's just that you can't take two
steps without getting goosed all the time . . .

HELENE:

Hey, ya want me to tell you something? I don't
know of one waitress who ever got anywhere without
a good share of goosing along the way . . .

28

MADO: *stops her manicure*
> Oh, come off it, right there! Now you're really
> shovellin' it! In the first place, I can't imagine how
> anybody'd manage to get herself goosed at Kresge's!
> They've got the girls all fenced in behind the counter!

HELENE: *laughing*
> Well, Kresge's wasn't exactly the height of my career,
> either . . .

MADO:
> Ah! If you mean St. Lawrence Street, well that's
> another matter! You have to admit there's a bit of
> a difference between a club on the Main and a cafe on
> Papineau Street! Myself, I never worked on the Main,
> but just the same, I've worked myself up to . . . oh . . .

> *She looks for words*

HELENE:
> Never mind, we know what you've worked yourself
> up to, baby. Nick didn't put you on the cash for
> nothin' . . .

LISE:
> Huh? Is that true? I didn't know that! Is that true,
> Mado?

MADO:
> You know, Lise, I think you're cute, I really do.
> Hélène hasn't been here as long as you, but she's
> already put the whole thing together! You're such
> an innocent!

LISE:
> Oh . . . But it's funny . . . I never would have thought . . .

MADO:

> Because Nick is running after you? That doesn't
> bother me, Lise, that doesn't bother me at all.

> *She looks LISE in the eyes.*

> As long as you keep sayin' no.

> *HELENE leans over to LISE.*

HELENE:

> Do you want me to tell you somethin', Lise, in all
> honesty now? I don't think you're cut out to be a
> waitress. I was just saying to Mado about it the
> other day, wasn't I, Mado? I was saying, "You know
> I don't think it's the best thing for Lise to stay on
> here. It's not for her . . . She's too different from the
> rest of us. It's just not working out at all." Why
> don't you see if you can't get on someplace else,
> salesgirl in a department store or something? Wouldn't
> you like that? I think you'd find that kind of work
> a lot better than this. A hundred times better.

> *MADO, visibly disgusted by this little ploy of
> HELENE's, stands up.*

MADO:

> I'm gonna go see if they've made any more of the
> special . . . There was none left at noon . . .

HELENE: *after MADO has left*

> Besides, Nick has his eye on you, and you don't seem
> too keen on goin' out with him . . . You're engaged,
> I know, that's your own business . . . But at any rate,
> Lise, if you don't give him what he's after, you won't
> have a job here for very long . . . And if you do give
> him what he wants, then you'll have Mado against
> you . . . And you'd have a real hell of a time trying to

get used to another waitress job. You remember what an awful time you had when you started at this place? Now, mind you, I wasn't here but Mado told me all about it. From what I hear it sounds like it was no picnic . . .

LISE bursts into tears.

HELENE:

There, there now, listen, don't start bawling, listen, what I'm saying, it's for your own good. It's not for myself, you know I don't have anything against working with you . . . You or anybody else, it's all the same to me. I'm just thinking about you, that's all. As far as that goes, the only reason I'm here is I'm just waiting for something better to turn up over on the Main. I'm not after your job, no, I'm speaking to you as a friend, Lise, and a little friendly advice never hurt anybody . . . I know just what you need . . . A nice peaceful little job behind a hosiery counter, or maybe in the cosmetics.

LISE:

Well, maybe you're right . . . But I'd be making a lot less money in a department store . . .

HELENE:

Well, you're engaged, you'll be getting married . . . You will, won't you? You told us you were engaged?

LISE:

Yes . . . At least, well . . . I left home six months ago to go live with André . . .

HELENE:

Ah! Yeah . . . Now I see . . . What does he do?

LISE:

He's . . . Well . . . He's looking for a job . . . He hasn't worked for quite a while . . .

HELENE:
>So that means . . . It's you that brings home the
>money!

>*LISE nods a yes.*

>How old is he, this boy?

LISE:
>Twenty-two.

HELENE:
>Good lookin'?

LISE:
>Oh, yeah, really good looking!

HELENE:
>You've been workin' ever since you been together?

>*LISE doesn't answer.*

>*HELENE looks at her for a few seconds.*

HELENE: *softly, reflectively*
>I know, I've been through that one myself . . .

>*She collects herself.*

>That's what you oughta do . . . If you go get yourself
>a job someplace that pays less, he'll have to go out
>and make some money! Look, here's a customer for
>you . . .

>*MADO returns.*

HELENE:

Here, take a napkin and blow your nose. Mado, you
better get back to the cash . . . Hurry up. If Nick
catches us gabbing with a customer waiting . . .

MADO gives her a dirty look.

MADO:

I know how to handle Nick, honey, don't worry!

HELENE:

Do you want me to fill in for you today, Lise? You're
an awful sight like that.

LISE: *blowing her nose*
If you like . . .

HELENE:

Good, ok, just for today we'll trade sections. I'll take
the big tables up front. You stay back here and have
a little rest. Look out, here comes Nick. Fold your
napkins. Hey, Nick, I'm taking Lise's place this
afternoon . . . She's got a bit of a headache . . .

MADO takes her by the arm, stops her.

MADO:

I can see the game you're playing with Lise, and I'm
stayin' out of it, it's none of my business . . . It's her
job you're after, isn't it? . . . Ok, maybe Lise isn't cut
out to be a waitress . . . Maybe she'll be leaving . . .
But if you take her place, honey, just watch yourself,
eh?! I wasn't born yesterday, and nobody cuts in
on me! Just remember, there's two things around
here that are hands off to you — Nick and the cash!
Got it?!

*HELENE, her mouth open, watches MADO
move away.*

33

LISE goes to the phone, puts in a dime, and dials a number.

LISE:

Hello . . . Hello, André? It's me . . . I've got something really important to tell you . . .

HELENE:

One smoke meat lean, pickles and mustard! One coffee, two creams.

MADO:

One thirty-seven!

LISE:

It took me a while to decide, but, you know, I just didn't know what to do. I was so miserable . . .

HELENE:

Two soup o' the day. Two club sand! One no mayo, one no bacon. Heavy on the mustard. Two cokes!

MADO:

Three fifty-six!

LISE:

Listen, André, don't talk to me like that, please! . . .

HELENE:

One smoke meat fat with pickles, one ham sand, salad and! One stack o' butter, one chocolate shake!

MADO:

Two twenty-eight!

LISE:

I know that, André, but I don't belong here. I'm going to try to get on someplace else, doing sales-clerking . . . At Greenberg's maybe, they're always needing help there . . .

HELENE:

Two hamburger platters with three relish and hold
the cold slaw. One cheese sand plain with mayo. One
caramel sundae no cherry, one chocolate cake à la
mode. Two cokes and a seven . . .

MADO:

Four and a quarter!

LISE:

Yes, I know I probably won't be making quite as
much to start with . . .

HELENE:

One hot dog with the works!

MADO:

Twenty cents!

LISE:

But I won't be so on edge all the time, think about
that! I'm at the end of my rope, you were just
saying so yourself the other day . . . My nerves are
all shot . . .

HELENE:

One grill cheese, one order toast, two coffees!

MADO:

One thirty-six.

LISE:

André . . . André . . . Don't hang up!

HELENE:

One cherry cola!

MADO:

Thirty-five cents!

LISE:

    André!

HELENE:

    One lemon pie, one glass of milk.

MADO:

    Seventy-five cents!

LISE:

    André!

HELENE:

    Two cokes, one pepsi, two seven-ups . . .

MADO:

    One dollar!

LISE:

    André . . . André, don't hang up . . . If you want me
    to I'll stay here, I'll stay here, if you want . . . André
    . . . I'll stay here . . . I'll stay here . . .

    She hangs up.

    Rhythmic music to accompany the following.

ALL THREE GIRLS:

    One smoke meat lean pickles and mustard. One coffee
    two creams. Two club sand, one no mayo, one no
    bacon, heavy on the mustard! Two cokes! One smoke
    meat fat with pickles, one ham sand, salad and mayo,
    one stack o' butter, one chocolate shake. Two
    hamburger platters with three relish, hold the cold
    slaw. One cheese sand plain with mayo. One caramel
    sundae no cherry, one chocolate cake à la mode. Two

cokes and a seven. One hot dog with the works. One
grill cheese, one stack o' brown, two coffees! One
cherry cola! One lemon pie, one glass of milk! Two
cokes, one pepsi, one seven-up! One pepper steak
hold the pepper, one spaghetti and meat balls, two
glasses of milk! One order sweet and sour! One
chicken in the basket and three honeys!

three

The bar of the "Coconut Inn."

LUCILLE, the barmaid, is on the house phone.

LUCILLE:
> No, he's not back yet. I don't know when. Yeah,
> yeah, I took care of everything. Mm-hm . . . Ok . . .
> Look, Betty, it was up to you to look after that!
> Next time you'll run your own errands, eh! Ah, save
> it for later, wouldya?!

> *She hangs up.*

As if I had nothin' else to do!

> *LUCILLE is the perfect example of the club
> waitress who's gone to the top. She has finally
> made it from the "floor" to the bar by pulling
> whatever strings, but her "superiority" exudes
> through every pore. She is very beautiful, but
> it is as if her beauty had not really blossomed
> until she had become "The barmaid of the
> Coconut Inn" . . .*

All her gestures are habitually precise, sure, calculated, confident. The presence of HELENE on the premises, however, disturbs her greatly, but she succeeds in retaining her calm nevertheless . . .

LUCILLE is exactly *what HELENE would have liked to become. This must also be evident in HELENE's face: envy and admiration in the same expression.*

LUCILLE turns to her glass washer who is trying to keep busy.

LUCILLE:
When you're through fakin' that you've got work to do there, you can go tell Toothpick I want to see him . . . About now he should be in the tavern across the street. Tell him I've got something for him . . .

During this time HELENE has come to sit down at the bar and watch LUCILLE "at work."

HELENE:
Forgotten our old friends already?

LUCILLE: *taken aback*
Huh?! . . . Hélène!

She freezes for a second.

What are you doing here?

HELENE:
Well how's that for a how-do-ya do? Come on, give me a scotch, and have one yourself, for old time's sake . . .

LUCILLE:
You know I don't drink on the job!

She doesn't move.

HELENE:
Ah, come on, get me a drink!

LUCILLE busies herself.

LUCILLE:
Hélène, I told you not to show your face around the
Coconut again. Are you crazy or what?

HELENE:
Aw, give me a break, Lucille, I'm off the hook now,
ain't I?!

LUCILLE: *cutting her off*
You're off the hook, but you're lucky you've got your
hide to show for it!

HELENE:
Don't give me that, Lucille . . .

LUCILLE:
With the money you owe Maurice, and the shit you
stirred up? I mean it, and I oughta know what I'm
talkin' about!

HELENE:
In other words, you're not exactly thrilled to see me!

LUCILLE:
Yes, I am, I am glad to see you . . . I mean, I would
be if we were any place else but here.

HELENE:
Oh, cut it out, what are you so nervous about?

LUCILLE:

Since when was I ever nervous? Look, baby, if I was the nervous type, I wouldn't be where I am today with the responsibilities I've got, ok? Listen, Hélène, I know about everything Maurice is mixed up in on the Main . . .

HELENE:

Alright, alright . . .

LUCILLE:

Well then take my advice . . . And get your ass outa here, fast! They haven't forgotten, Hélène, you better believe it!

HELENE: *raising her voice*

Well I haven't forgotten either, dammit, think about that for a minute! I haven't forgotten the dirty deal they handed me!

LUCILLE:

The difference is, baby, they're the ones runnin' the show, not you! Please, Hélène, go along home now, eh, and give me a buzz tomorrow, I've got the day off . . . You can come over to the house and I'll make up a batch of spaghetti . . .

HELENE:

I wanna see you tonight, Lucille!

LUCILLE:

Were you drinking before you came down here?

HELENE:

Uh-uh, not a drop . . .

LUCILLE turns to her dishwasher.

She hasn't realized he has ducked out while she was talking.

LUCILLE:
>Never mind about Toothpick, Louis . . . Ah, he's
>gone already! You'd better down that scotch in a
>hurry, Hélène. Toothpick's on his way over!

>>*HELENE looks automatically towards the
>>door. She finishes the scotch in one gulp.*

HELENE:
>Toothpick don't scare me! Give me another scotch,
>Lucille . . .

LUCILLE:
>No, I'm sure you had something before you got here
>. . . You know what scotch does to you, Hélène . . .
>You can't hold your liquor anymore . . .

HELENE:
>I can't hold my liquor anymore? Is this my best
>friend I hear, tellin' me I can't hold my liquor? I can
>hold down a goddam twenty-sixer and still walk a
>straight line!

>>*She takes the bottle that LUCILLE has left on
>>the counter and pours herself a brimming glass-
>>ful of scotch.*

HELENE: *clearly separating her syllables*
>For old times' sake, Lucille!

LUCILLE:
>I shouldn't even bother with you . . . I should let
>you guzzle yourself under the table, and then let
>them haul you off, like the last time . . .

HELENE:
>The cops?

LUCILLE:
>No, not the cops . . . The best thing that can happen
>to you when you get plastered, Hélène, is for the
>cops to pull you in. At least they're not dangerous . . .

>*She takes HELENE's hand.*

>You've always been a friend, Hélène. You're almost a
>sister to me! Hell, we both grew up in the same back
>alley! That's why I protected you all I could the time
>they kicked you out in the street!

HELENE:
>Don't give me the mother hen routine . . .

LUCILLE: *hiding the bottle*
>If I hadn't done anything for you last year, you know
>where you'd be now, Hélène?

HELENE: *looking LUCILLE in the eye.*
>Yeah, I know where I'd be. And I'd be a helluva lot
>better off than I am slingin' smoked meat on Papineau
>Street, Lucille!

LUCILLE:
>Just cool it for a while, Hélène, and don't go doing
>anything stupid . . . Hang on for . . . A year, say . . .
>And then I'll see what I can do for you . . . Keep on
>paying what you owe to Maurice . . .

HELENE:
>I can't wait a year . . . And I'm not making enough to
>pay Maurice. You understand?

>*LUCILLE, affected by this, doesn't answer*
>*right away. HELENE empties her second glass.*

HELENE:
>One more . . . Come on, one more!

LUCILLE:
> I've got every reason in the world to hate you, after
> what you did to me, and I just can't . . . But them . . .

> *The phone rings. LUCILLE and HELENE jump,*
> *look at the phone, then each other. LUCILLE*
> *picks up the receiver.*

LUCILLE:
> Hello? . . . Ah, it's you . . .

> *HELENE looks at the door again. She is*
> *beginning to get drunk.*

LUCILLE:
> No, no, everything's ok . . . Where are you now?

> *She jumps.*

> You're back already? When are you coming in? Ah . . .
> Ok . . . No, I told you everything's fine . . . Ok, bye.

> *She hangs up.*

> This isn't your day . . . Maurice is back from his trip
> . . . He's on his way over.

HELENE:
> Maurice? Good, it'll be a pleasure doing business
> with him!

LUCILLE:
> Hélène! You don't think you're gonna stay here!

HELENE:
> Sure I am! And I'm gonna hit him up for a twenty.
> That way, he'll know just how broke I am . . . Let
> him take me back on here, then I'll be able to pay
> back what I owe him!

HELENE: *whispering*
And he'd lay off my mother too . . .

LUCILLE:
He'll never take you back on here! I'll try to get you
on somewhere else, next year, but not here! You
tried to get my job, last year, Hélène, and they
busted you one in the mouth for it! You think I
don't know you were trying to get my job? You did
everything you could to get Maurice against me, and
then when he realized there wasn't a bit of truth in
what you were saying . . . Hélène, you're not listening!
You've got a habit of doing that when a person has
something important to say to you . . .

The phone rings again.

Not again, who's it gonna be this time!?

HELENE:
If it's Maurice, tell him I send him a nice big kiss!
Well, I've got a right, haven't I?

LUCILLE:
Hello? Yeah, it's me . . . Yeah . . . About three
hundred and fifty . . . Well, I'm sorry, I can't perform
miracles! It's a Monday, you know . . .

Pauses.

My place? Are you crazy? I can't take that up to
my place! Yeah, I know . . . Ok . . . But this is the
last time, just remember that!

*She hangs up. She pushes a button near the
phone.*

The Master of Ceremonies comes onto the stage.

HELENE:
>Hey, Shorty is still here, eh? He's havin' a drink too, and I don't see you kickin' him out!

M.C.:
>Merci, mesdames et messieurs, merci . . . Fantastic, eh, aren't they just fantastic though?

>*Feeble applause.*

>A big hand now, mesdames et messieurs, a big hand for our sensational band here, "Big Jack and the Jokers!" The swingingest boys in town, les gars les plus swingeux en ville . . . Yes sir, let's hear it again folks. Big Jack, you are the most! And now, mesdames et messieurs, it is with great pride and satisfaction in our hearts that the Coconut Inn has the honour of presenting to you, just back from their triumphant tour which has taken them to the four corners of la belle provence, direct from Chibougamau, here they are, your stars of tomorrow, the beautiful, the talented, "The Aurora Sisters!"

HELENE:
>The what?

LUCILLE:
>The Aurora Sisters . . .

HELENE:
>They any good?

LUCILLE:
>Aw, I dunno . . . I've seen my fill of these numbers . . . They're something different though . . .

THE AURORA SISTERS: *singing*
>Now Hélène left her home to be on her own,
>Off to try out her wings, and she should have known.
>When her wings, they were spread, she began to sing —
>And fell right on her face, poor thing!

So girls, beware! You'll get no pity
From that cold, cold-hearted city;
Don't you leave your Ma's and Pa's,
Your cousins and all your in-laws!

HELENE:
Lucille . . . Lucille . . . If you only knew! This is
where I belong, Lucille! This is the only place I can
be happy!

THE AURORA SISTERS:
Well, Hélène, she came home and without a word
Moped around like a sadder but a wiser bird;
All the fine, pretty feathers upon her wings
Were burnt to a crisp, poor things!

So girls, beware! You'll get no pitty
From that cold, cold-hearted city;
Don't you leave your Ma's and Pa's,
Your cousins and all your in-laws!

HELENE:
I can't go on hustlin' smoked meat, I just can't do it
anymore! It's the clubs I need, rue St. Laurent, the
nighttime! I've always been a nightowl, Lucille!
I love it!

THE AURORA SISTERS:
Now Hélène stays at home and she mends her wings
Patiently for to see what the future brings,
'Cause she hopes that her wings, if she only waits,
Will get her to the pearly gates!

So girls, beware! You'll get no pity
From that cold, cold-hearted city;
Don't you leave your Ma's and Pa's,
Your cousins and all your in-laws!

Feeble applause.

HELENE:

Couldn't I just sit here all night and watch you work?
I don't wanna go back home! Lucille, just let me stay
here, I'll be quiet!

*PAUL, the caretaker of the Coconut Inn,
arrives.*

PAUL:

Lucille, my love, you rang for me? I didn't come right
away, I wanted to hear the song . . . It's my favourite
part of the act . . .

LUCILLE:

Lucky for you I wasn't in a hurry, eh?

*She gives PAUL a very small package and some
keys.*

PAUL:

Well, get a load o' this, if it isn't Hélène! How are
you, gorgeous? Long time no see, eh?

HELENE: *dryly*

Just fine, thanks. Couldn't be better!

She turns her back on him.

PAUL:

Still as sweet as ever! A barking dog is liable to get
bit some day, baby . . .

LUCILLE:

Go take this into Maurice's office, Paul. And bring
me back the keys, eh?

HELENE:

Lucille! Let me just sit here, I'll be quiet as anything!

*At this instant, she sees TOOTHPICK in the
mirror of the bar, who has just come in. He
approaches slowly, a broad grin on his face,
a toothpick planted between his teeth.*

He is short, thin, with a cheap, phoney elegance.

LUCILLE:
Pull yourself together, Hélène. Don't get stupid!

*TOOTHPICK doesn't dare sit down beside
HELENE. He stays three or four seats away from
her.*

TOOTHPICK:
Hi, Hélène. Come to give us a bad time?

*HELENE is content to just look at him. She
doesn't speak.*

LUCILLE:
Hélène came to see me, it's none of your business,
Toothpick . . .

TOOTHPICK:
To borrow a five off you, I guess, eh? Don't you
owe enough as it is?

LUCILLE:
You stay outa this, smartass. I told you, it's none
o' your business!

TOOTHPICK:
Damn well is my business! Maruice told me to keep
an eye on you while he was away . . .

LUCILLE:
Well, he's back now, Maurice is, he just called. He's
coming down. So I don't need you anymore . . .

And besides, I can't see Maurice telling you to keep an eye on me . . . Have you ever even talked to Maurice, you little punk?

TOOTHPICK:
Maurice? We're buddies! Yeah, we're like that, me an' Maurice!

Holding up two fingers together.

We work for each other . . .

LUCILLE:
You mean *you* work for him . . . Doing his cheap dirty work . . .

TOOTHPICK:
Like babysitting you, for example . . . Hey, was it you just sent for me? Well, what did you want?

LUCILLE:
Never mind, it's not important. You can come back later . . . And don't talk to me in that tone of voice, you little bastard!

TOOTHPICK, playing the big-shot, comes to sit down beside HELENE.

TOOTHPICK:
How's your little brother Marcel, Hélène? Still sick in his little head? Last time I saw him, he was pretty well out to lunch, wasn't he? Looks like you're not doin' so bad yourself, still drinking like a fish? You keep that up, I guess it won't be long before you'll be packin' off to join him, eh?

He grins broadly. HELENE spits in his face. TOOTHPICK, too frightened to hit HELENE, who is bigger than him anyway, contents himself with laughing stupidly while he wipes his face.

TOOTHPICK: *chewing on his toothpick*
You're gonna pay for this, Hélène, you're gonna pay
plenty for this! Your little brother might be hearin'
from us real soon!

He goes off.

LUCILLE:
You think that was smart, what you just did?

HELENE:
Yes.

LUCILLE:
You'd better take off and fast . . . Toothpick's just a
punk, but he's got friends . . .

HELENE:
I know. And I don't give a shit! It's ok, I'm going
now . . . I don't want you to get into any trouble
on account of me . . . Hey, Lucille, could you spare
me a five? I'm going down to the Casa Istanbul, they
won't look for me there . . .

*LUCILLE opens the cash register and gives
her a five.*

LUCILLE:
I'll call you, tomorrow . . . Go out the back way . . .

HELENE:
No. I've never gone out the back way, and I'm not
starting now! So long, Lucille, you're a good kid . . .
Yeah, you're ok . . .

*She goes away from the bar and comes up face
to face with MAURICE. MAURICE is the big
boss of the Coconut Inn. Dressed like a prince,
sharp, flashy, pearl in the tie, etc.*

MAURICE: *smiling*
    Hi there, Hélène.

        From his manner of speaking we see that
        TOOTHPICK was imitating him just a while
        ago.

    I just bumped into Toothpick. I'm gonna look the
other way, for tonight, I haven't got time to be
bothered with you . . . I've got more urgent business
to take care of . . . I'm just gonna forget that I saw
you. But don't come back here, I'm warning you . . .
Never!

HELENE:
    You don't scare me, Maurice.

MAURICE: *takes her by the wrist*
    No? What about at home, do I scare *them*? Go on,
get outa here! Go get yourself pissed somewhere else.

        HELENE leaves. MAURICE comes up, rests
        his elbows on the bar.

LUCILLE:
    It's ok, Maurice, I'll never mention Hélène again . . .

        Music.

four

The courtyard.

MME. BELANGER: *finishing her coke, she makes a slurping
noise with the straws*
You can take my word for it . . . That Hélène's about
washed up for good . . . Well, that's her own tough
luck, I guess; she's been askin' for it since God knows
when . . .

MME. L'HEUREUX:
Her mother, she's hidin' behind her Venetian blinds
over there, just waitin' for her. Been waiting her
whole life long. She'll rot behind those blinds . . .

MME. GINGRAS:
Used to be her husband she'd be waitin' for . . . Every
other Friday night he'd come home juiced to the gills
with another woman on his arm . . . Hand the wife
over a few bucks so's her and the kids wouldn't
starve . . .

MME. L'HEUREUX:
> These days instead of the old man it's Hélène comes in raisin' hell and swearin' to beat the band . . .

MME. TREMBLAY:
> And then there's a scene . . .

MME. MONETTE:
> Every time Hélène comes home plastered they have a scene. It's like . . . Like an obligation, you might say . . .

MME. BEAULIEU:
> Like a craving!

ALL THE WOMEN:
> They can't help themselves, they love it!

MME. MONETTE:
> When that bunch gets a battle goin', they can be at it till the next morning . . . That is if Hélène can stand up that long.

MME. DANSEREAU:
> If Hélène is too far gone, the old bat can knock her out with a swift clout, and haul her off to bed.

MME. L'HEUREUX:
> Next morning Hélène gets up, calm, collected, sweet as pie . . .

MME. GINGRAS:
> Doesn't remember a thing . . . Her mother doesn't mention anything . . . Or Henri . . . Or the daughter, Francine . . . Well that Francine, she never opens her mouth anyway . . . Couldn't say boo to a grasshopper, that one . . . Always has been a bit of a stick-in-the-mud . . .

MME. MONETTE:
   And then the same night, if Hélène comes in loaded,
   they start all over again!

   The women laugh.

ALL THE WOMEN:
   They can't help themselves, they love it!

MME. JOANETTE:
   Sometimes . . . Sometimes there's these men come to
   pay a visit to the old lady on a Saturday morning . . .
   Three of them usually . . . One stays in the car and
   the other two go up and knock on the back door . . .
   They always talk in whispers . . .

MME. MENARD:
   She always looks scared stiff of them . . . Once I heard
   her raise her voice . . . She'd been arguing with them
   about something for a couple of minutes . . . Then all
   of a sudden she yells out, "You can do what you
   like with me, but don't you lay a hand on them!
   They're my children, after all." Then she goes into
   the house for a minute, comes back out and slips
   them a twenty . . .

   The women start to laugh.

MME. L'HEUREUX:
   Hélène's later than usual gettin' home tonight,
   Joseph . . .

MME. GINGRAS:
   If you ask me, I think we're gonna have ourselves
   a show after all . . .

   The women laugh louder and louder.

   Music.

five

Robertine's living room.

*A very poor, very shabby living room. The
furniture is threadbare. Even the television is
twelve or thirteen years old.*

*ROBERTINE and FRANCINE are playing
"Crazy Eights" on the living room coffee table.
HENRI is sprawled in an armchair watching
cartoons on TV.*

*ROBERTINE is short, wizened. She is dressed
in an old housecoat. She is arthritic and has
much difficulty moving her hands. Her gestures
are always a little awkward.*

*FRANCINE is fifteen. She is very pretty, but
her face betrays a kind of hardness. She hardly
ever speaks, but she sees all.*

*HENRI should be the epitome of the failure,
the mediocre freeloader. He has never done anything, has always, or almost always, lived off*

Hélène, and now that old age threatens him (he is forty-five), he is just letting himself go rather than fighting it. We feel that he was handsome once, but only passingly. He may have started to get old at thirty . . .

ROBERTINE:

Your mother sure is taking her time!

FRANCINE:

What time did she say she was coming home?

ROBERTINE:

Well, she's supposed to be off work at five . . . She said she'd come right home . . .

HENRI:

Francine, come and watch the cartoons.

FRANCINE:

Do you think maybe . . . ?

HENRI:

Come over here, Francine. Come and see the cartoons.

ROBERTINE:

I wouldn't be surprised. That's usually where she is when she's this late . . .

HENRI:

Popeye's on. Come and watch Popeye, Francine . . .

ROBERTINE:

I knew she'd fall back on her old ways . . . It's been a while since she's been down at the clubs . . .

FRANCINE:

It's your turn.

ROBERTINE:

What?

FRANCINE:

> The cards, it's your turn. I put down the four and you put down the Jack . . .

ROBERTINE:

> Ah . . . I just don't have a head for cards today . . .

HENRI:

> Come and see Popeye, Francine. Popeye's on. Come and watch him.

FRANCINE:

> Ok, ok, I heard you the first time, Daddy. Do you have to repeat everything five hundred times?

HENRI:

> Well, it's Popeye . . .

ROBERTINE:

> Honestly Henri, you can be so damned annoying sometimes. Can't you just keep quiet for a while?

HENRI:

> Well, I wanted Francine to see Popeye. It's her favourite. Eh, Francine, you always watch Popeye, don't you? Sure she does, she used to be crazy about cartoons. We always watch Captain Cartoons together, don't we? . . .

FRANCINE:

> Oh, shut up, Daddy! Just shut up, you're getting on my nerves.

HENRI: *on purpose*

> Captain Cartoons and all his animals! I kind of like Popeye myself. He gobbles that old spinach down there, and then he grows those muscles, like that . . .

ROBERTINE:

> Henri, we don't feel like hearing the life story of Popeye again!

61

HENRI:

Look, now he's over. You missed Popeye, Francine.
But Captain Cartoons isn't finished yet . . . They'll
have some more, maybe more Popeyes. Ah! . . . Look
Francine, there he is, Captain Cartoons! Howdy, there,
Captain Cartoons! How's it goin'?

ROBERTINE:

I swear, ever since he started talking to the TV set,
I just . . .

HENRI:

Well, I'm gonna get a beer.

He seems to have great difficulty standing up.

HENRI:

Where did you go and put my cane, Francine? Where's
my cane?

FRANCINE:

Don't ask me. I haven't seen your cane. You had it
when you came to sit down.

HENRI:

I can't find it.

ROBERTINE:

Well, just have a good look for it!

HENRI:

I don't know why it's not here! It should be! You've
hidden it on me, haven't you? You don't want me to
get up! That's it, isn't it? You don't want me to get
up!

ROBERTINE:

Oh, for heaven's sake, Henri, to think the child'd be
tryin' to hide your cane on you! Not that I'm not
tempted to myself once in a while, to keep you from
gettin' up in the morning . . .

FRANCINE has gotten up and found the cane under the armchair.

FRANCINE:
> Here's your cane. You can quit your hollering now.

HENRI:
> You were hiding it on me . . .

ROBERTINE:
> Oh come on, Henri. You know damn well she wasn't hiding it on you. You let it roll under the chair on purpose. You're always doing that just to give yourself something to gripe about. It gets awfully tiresome you know, Henri. And then you think we don't realize you're taking us all for a bunch of fools. Why don't you just give up on this making out like you're worse off than you are!

HENRI:
> What? What's that? What are you talking about?

FRANCINE:
> Oh, now he goes into his "what are you talking about" routine . . .

HENRI:
> I'm going to get a beer . . .

> *Before leaving the living room he turns to his mother-in-law and starts to sing.*

> I'm Popeye the sailor man . . . I'm Popeye the sailor man . . .

> *He exits.*

ROBERTINE:
> That's it, that's it, go hide away in the kitchen. Well this time nobody can be bothered goin' out to look for you.

FRANCINE:

He's getting worse every day. He didn't used to be that bad.

ROBERTINE:

Well, your father never has been overly bright.

FRANCINE:

No, I know, but that was just terrible. It's getting so you can't live with him, that's all there is to it!

ROBERTINE:

Well, you know how he is. He does it all on purpose. He just puts it on . . . Oh, I'm too tired to play any more "Crazy Eights" right now. My nerves are all on edge.

FRANCINE:

Do you want to play something else?

ROBERTINE:

No. I've got a headache. As usual.

She sighs.

Well, I think I'll make myself a cup of tea. If your mother ever gets home, I'm gonna have a fine time of it. If only she wouldn't get it into her head to go on these binges . . .

FRANCINE:

She'd be home by now if she was sober, Grandma. I think we're gonna be in for some trouble tonight . . .

ROBERTINE:

Oh, and I'm so tired. Not tired like . . . Oh, I don't know . . . Fed up is what I mean . . . I'm just fed up with it all . . . Always the same thing over and over! She's alright for two or three months, and all of a sudden . . . It blows up again . . . *And* the screaming, *and* the name calling . . . Do you want some tea? Oh,

that's right, you don't drink tea, do you? I'm going to
go set the table. Maybe she'll be hungry . . . I'll send
your father in . . .

She exits.

*HELENE comes staggering into the courtyard.
She is completely plastered. She sees the women,
who are watching her without acknowledging
her.*

HELENE:
Well, well, so the whole barnyard's out to roost
already! Hi, girls! Good weather for hangin' out
the wash eh?!

She sees MME. L'HEUREUX.

Still got your nose caught in the blinds, Carmen?

She looks at Robertine's window.

Good thing Mother's got hers down . . .

Before going in, she turns to the women.

Don't worry, you're gonna hear it all anyway!

She goes into the house.

FRANCINE:
Ah, here you are . . . We've been waiting for you
since five o'clock . . .

HELENE:
Well, if it isn't my little Francine! Ooooooo!!

*She goes over to FRANCINE and tries to
kiss her.*

FRANCINE pushes her away.

65

FRANCINE:
>Oh, Mother . . .

HELENE:
>What's the matter? Don't you wanna give your
>mother a kiss? Come on now. You haven't given
>your mother a little kiss for ages . . . Come on. Just
>a little peck. I'm your own mother, aren't I?

FRANCINE:
>You smell like a brewery!

HELENE:
>Oh, so I do, do I? Well, so what! Ain't I got a right
>to go out and have a bit of fun once in a while?
>Alright, so I have had a few. I felt like going for a
>drink and I did. It's a free country, ain't it? Who
>asked for your opinion anyway? You trying to tell
>me I can't take a drink now and then? Well, nobody
>tells me I can't take a drink when I want to! The
>bastard ain't been born yet that tells Hélène she
>can't take a drink when she wants to. Ok?!

ROBERTINE: *from the kitchen*
>Is that you, Hélène?

HELENE:
>Well, well, and how's that little silver haired mother
>o' mine? Yes, dear, it's me. Hélène, your little girl.
>Are you glad to see me? Wait a minute, I'm coming
>right out to the kitchen to talk to you.

>*She bumps her knee on the coffee table.*

>Goddam that fuckin' table anyway. Put that thing
>back where it belongs, Francine, before I wrap it
>around your neck!

She exits. During the conversation that takes place in the kitchen, a room which we don't see, HENRI comes out to the living room and sits down in front of the TV. FRANCINE slowly picks up the cards HELENE has thrown on the floor.

HELENE:

Hi there, Mother! How's it going, eh? Did you have a nice day? Are you glad to see me? It's me, your daughter, Hélène. Don't you recognize me? What are you doing, making yourself a cup of tea? T.E.A. Tea? You're a regular little tea granny, aren't you? A little tea'll do you good just before supper, eh?

She laughs.

And how's your arthritis today? Just the same? Poor Mummy . . . Hey, you know what you need? Tea's no good for ya, you should try a twenty-sixer o' gin . . .

ROBERTINE:

Would you shut up!? Keep your drunken foolery to yourself, why don't you? Do you think that's smart, eh? Do you think that's a smart thing to do, coming home soused up to the eyeballs like this?

HELENE:

So what?! I was having fun. I was only having a little fun, Mother. Do you hold that against me? Do you hold that against your own daughter?

ROBERTINE:

Look out where you're waving your arms there, you're gonna have me spilling this boiling water in a minute. I don't feel like scalding myself on top of everything else!

FRANCINE goes to sit beside her father. They do not move.

HELENE:

> Yeah, that's it, now go and accuse me of trying to burn you. And then tell all the neighbours, like you always do!

ROBERTINE:

> Let me get by there . . . I'm going into the living room . . .

HELENE:

> That's it, run away. That's you alright! Well, it doesn't bother me none. I'm coming in after you . . . I'm just going to the john for a minute and I'll be right out.

> > *A door is heard closing. ROBERTINE comes into the living room with her cup of tea. The cup of tea is very important since ROBERTINE uses it as much to warm her hands as to drink from.*

ROBERTINE:

> The same thing . . . The same thing all over again . . . Never fails! For years I've had to put up with that . . . And never say a word! I've earned my eternal rest, I'll tell you, have I ever. And it looks like she's in one of her worst moods tonight. Francine, you've got to help me . . . We've got to try and reason with her or . . . Ah, no, that won't do any good. I guess we'll just have to sit and take it all and keep quiet. The curses and the names and the accusations and the making up again . . . What a prospect for an evening! I almost feel like packing up and walking out.

> > *FRANCINE, stunned at this, looks at her grandmother.*

> No, no, you know I wouldn't leave you alone in the house with her. She's liable to kill you, you and your father both. Although, as far as your father goes, I wouldn't . . .

HENRI looks over at ROBERTINE.

Well, what do you know, you caught on that time! . . .

A toilet flushes. A door opens and closes.

Here comes the hurricane again.

HELENE:
>Well, well, and here's my darling husband! My Tarzan!
>Just look at him! Now is that or isn't that a gorgeous
>hunk of man! A real killer! Hey, Henri! It's me. Are
>you glad to see me? Hey, hey Henri, show me your
>muscles. Come on! Let's see them! Look here,
>Francine. Just feel that! You'd think it was Charles
>Atlas in person. Are you gonna give your little Hélène
>a nice smoochie-smooch on the cheek, Tarzan? Come
>on, go ahead! Just a little peck!

>*She sits on HENRI and kisses him.*

>He can't even kiss properly any more, the bastard!
>Look at him! He's so scared he's shitting in his pants!
>You lazy good for nothing! You louse! You imbecile!
>Can't you see yourself? You look like a cockroach,
>you know that!? No, not even that. You're too slow
>for a cockroach!

ROBERTINE:
>Hélène! . . .

HELENE:
>Would you look at that! That there is my husband!
>I married that thing fourteen years ago! Fourteen
>years I've put up with this clod! And I keep him
>alive because he can't go out and get a job!

ROBERTINE:
>Hélène! . . .

HELENE:
>Don't look at me like that, you, or I'm liable to paste
>you one right in the mouth! You, over there, watch
>your cartoons! Go ahead, watch your stupid Captain
>Cartoons and talk to the TV screen like a two-year
>old. To think I thought I was in love with that retard!

ROBERTINE:
>Hélène, cut it out!

HELENE:
>To think I married that louse because he was good
>looking. Ha, ha! Jesus, was I ever crazy!

ROBERTINE:
>Hélène, the neighbours'll be listening!

HELENE:
>Well, of course the neighbours are listening! They've
>got nothin' else better to do, have they? They've
>been spying on us for twenty years!

ROBERTINE:
>Alright, alright, but you don't have to shout at the
>top of your lungs like that!

HELENE:
>Ah, well, shut up yourself, why don't you?! Go
>blubber in the corner and drink your tea! That's
>about all you're good for! That's about all you can
>do, now that it's too late!

ROBERTINE:
>Hélène, don't you talk to me like that! I won't have
>it! And I was always so good to you!

HELENE: *bursts out laughing*
>Ha, that's a good one, that is! That's a real beauty!
>She was always so good to me! What did you ever
>do for me, eh? Tell me. Go on, let's just hear it!

ROBERTINE:

> I'm warning you, I'm not going to stand for anymore,
> Hélène!

HELENE:

> You're scared, eh? You're scared I might say some-
> thing. Just what did you ever do for me? When did
> you ever lift a finger to stop me from marrying that
> louse over there? Never! Never a goddam word.
> I was too young. I thought I was in love . . .

ROBERTINE:

> It was no use talking to you. You wouldn't have
> listened . . .

HELENE:

> Maybe not. But maybe I would have listened if you'd
> been a normal mother. But no, you were so stupid,
> so cheap, I was ashamed of you. And such a dummy!
> They don't even make 'em that dumb any more!
> You weren't even human in those days! A real weirdo!
> All my girlfriends were scared of you! Nobody could
> stand you! Worse than a moron! It's your fault
> everybody in this family's so goddam miserable! If
> you'd brought us up properly, I could have married
> somebody half decent, but no . . .

ROBERTINE:

> Aren't you ashamed of yourself talking like that to
> me? You don't know what you're saying, Hélène!
> Now stop it, right now!

HELENE:

> What do you mean I don't know what I'm saying?
> I fuckin' well do know! You never raised us like
> normal kids, Claude and me. Yeah, let's talk about
> Claude! Why don't we just have a little chat about
> Claude, my dear little kid brother Claude out in the
> sanatorium! Now, who was it made him that way,
> eh? Who was it?

blames
mother.

71

ROBERTINE:

> I won't have it, do you hear me? I won't have you
> talking about Claude like that! You've got no right,
> Hélène! You know it's not my fault he's like that
> today! Now be quiet! You'll say anything just to
> hurt me!

HELENE:

> Oh, so, you're scared, are you? You don't like to
> have anyone tell you the plain gospel truth. Well,
> you were never a mother to us. You never gave a
> damn about us and now you're playing the big martyr!
> Well, if you're sick these days, if it hurts you to
> squirm from one place to another, then you damn
> well deserve it! You're just lucky I keep you here
> to look after Francine!

ROBERTINE: *softly*

> You don't know what you're saying, Hélène. When
> you're sober you can be so nice! So nice! Why do
> you do it? Why do you get tanked up like this?
> Listen to me, Hélène, when you get drunk your
> thinking goes all haywire and the past gets mixed up
> in your head.

HELENE:

> That's not true! That's not true!

ROBERTINE:

> Yes, it is true! You know it's the truth! You know
> I told you not to marry Henri, that he was a good-for-
> nothing, but you went and married him anyway!

HELENE:

> That's not true!

ROBERTINE:

> You were crazy about him because he was good
> looking and all the girls were running after him, and
> rich bitches used to pick him up on Dorion Street,

and pay him to sleep with them! But you wanted him
all to yourself! So you got yourself pregnant to make
him marry you!

HELENE:

That's not true! That's not true!

ROBERTINE:

It is so true! When you get drinking you try to tell
everybody everything backwards and make me to
blame for you messing up your own life!

HELENE:

That's not true!

ROBERTINE:

Well I've had enough, do you understand me? I'm
fed up with it, once and for all! I'm fed up with
being taken for a madwoman on account of you.
If I didn't raise you properly it's because you just
weren't raisable!

HELENE:

That's not true!

ROBERTINE:

You were a hot tempered little brat is what you were!
If anybody said two words to you when you were
little you'd have a conniption fit! You'd go stiff as
a board and then slobber like a mad dog. You don't
remember that, eh?

HELENE:

No, I don't remember that!

ROBERTINE:

I guess you don't remember the scenes you used to
make when you were thirteen and wanted to stay out
after midnight either? I guess you don't remember

the time you went around telling the whole neighbourhood you loved niggers because their fat lips
were so good for kissing? I guess you don't
remember all the bruises you gave me?

HELENE:

No! That's not true! I wasn't hot tempered!! Henri,
stick up for me! Tell her I wasn't hot tempered! Tell
her she was hot tempered!

ROBERTINE:

And now you just finish telling me you were ashamed
of me. Well, it was your friends you were ashamed of,
Hélène! You didn't think I caught on to who they
were, did you? Those friends of yours? Well it was
me that was ashamed of you, Hélène! But I kept it
to myself. I made excuses for you left and right.
I don't know what I didn't do to keep people from
finding out about you, Hélène!

HELENE:

Henri, say something, stick up for me! Tell her I was
ashamed of her because she was so cheap!

ROBERTINE:

And you think you weren't cheap, you of all people!
When you'd come in at four in the morning and wake
all the neighbours up yelling and singing and swearing,
and you think that wasn't being cheap?! And then
you go and have the gall to talk to me about Claude!
To blame me for making him the way he is today
when you know very well he came into the world
like that and the doctor told us he'd never have the
mind of anymore than a four-year old boy. Do you
remember what he looked like when he was first
born, Hélène? Do you remember? Tell me you
remember how he looked! Tell me, Hélène! Tell me!

She takes HELENE by the arms and shakes her.

HELENE:
>No, no that's not true! I don't remember!

ROBERTINE:
>Tell me, Hélène! Tell me you were wrong!

HELENE:
>No! Let go, you're hurting me!

ROBERTINE:
>Tell me you remember him!

HELEN:
>No! No! No!

ROBERTINE:
>Tell me! Tell me!

HELENE:
>No! No!

ROBERTINE: *screaming*
>Tell me that I'm right, Hélène!

HELENE: *breaks down sobbing*
>Yes. Yes, you're right, I remember. Let go of me.
>I remember. I was wrong! I was wrong!

>*HELENE is on the floor at ROBERTINE's*
>*feet.*

ROBERTINE: *after a silence*
>Now, apologize to me!

HELENE:
>Yes. Yes, I apologize. You were right, I am a little
>bitch!

ROBERTINE:
>That was just awful, what you did tonight, Hélène . . .

HELENE:

Yes, that's true. It was just awful. I hate myself,
mother, I just hate myself. I'm a bitch, you're
absolutely right! You were always so good to me.
It was always my fault! I'm a rotten daughter! I just
did it all on purpose to make you suffer. I deserve
a good beating, Mother, I deserve a real good thrash-
ing! I'm so sorry! I'll never do it again! Never!
Never!

ROBERTINE:

Well, alright then, come along to bed. A good
sleep'll do you good.

HELENE:

Yes, yes that'll do me good. I'm so sorry.

ROBERTINE:

Come on. Come on . . .

HELENE:

Alright, but before I go to bed I want to have an
arm wrestle with Henri. Do you want one, Henri?
Do you wanna have an arm wrestle with me? Come
on, now! Well say something, answer me!

ROBERTINE:

Leave him alone, Hélène. This is no time to be arm
wrestling.

HELENE:

Ok, maybe not, but I would of beat him, you can be
sure of that! Oh, would I ever beat him, just you
watch . . .

ROBERTINE:

Yes, yes, alright, Hélène . . . You'd beat him, we
know . . .

HELENE:
>   Do you wanna have an arm wrestle with me, Henri?
>   Do you wanna have an arm wrestle? Eh? Do you . . . ?

ROBERTINE:
>   Come to bed, Hélène . . . Come on . . . Come to bed . . .

>   *HELENE and ROBERTINE exit.*

>   *FRANCINE looks at her father with a profound contempt.*

FRANCINE:
>   You didn't say anything. You didn't do a thing. Not even budge. You were scared! . . . You can sit up straight now, she's gone! Watch out for your cane, so it doesn't roll under the chair again . . .

>   *She gets up and goes to turn off the TV.*

>   *Music.*

six

The courtyard.

MME. BELANGER:

> Well, I guess that's the show over for another
> night . . . I'm gonna go in and get another coke . . .
> Maybe there'll be something good on TV . . . I'll
> come back out if there's any more action . . .

MME. L'HEUREUX:

> When Claude was first born and the old bat came
> home from the hospital, she didn't wanna show
> that kid to anybody! I don't think anybody saw hide
> nor hair o' that child before it was a year old . . . A
> couple of times word went round that he was dead,
> then all of a sudden you'd hear him howlin' on the
> other side of the yard . . .

MME. GINGRAS:

> Myself, I used to see her passing by the window once
> in a while . . . I could see that she was carrying
> *some*thing in her arms, but it certainly didn't look
> like any baby . . . I mean, it was too small . . . Like a

little animal . . . But I never could get a good look
at it 'cause soon as she caught me lookin', down went
the blinds . . .

MME. L'HEUREUX:
Then one fine day, the following spring it was, she
decided it was time to show him off. She barged
outa that house like a hurricane'd struck her, and
made the rounds of the neighbourhood with him.

MME. TREMBLAY:
That kid was a year old but it still looked like a
new-born baby.

MME. MENARD:
A real little monster it was too, with these beady
black eyes, no expression in 'em, kinda like kids'
marbles.

MME. MONETTE:
Every time I'd look at those eyes they'd give me the
creeps . . .

MME. L'HEUREUX:
That Claude always looked like he had it in for the
whole world . . . And when he got older he turned
into the meanest little cuss you ever seen . . . I mean,
nobody could go near him . . . He was always hiding
off in a corner, or under his mother's skirts . . . When
it came time to send him to school, well, there was
just no way to get him to go . . . He wasn't havin'
none of it.

MME. BELANAGER:
And it took them twenty years to realize that boy
was crazy!

MME. SOUCY:
Of course the whole neighbourhood knew it long
before, that he was crazy . . .

MME. MONETTE:

> Well, they must have known it themselves, but they didn't want to admit it . . .

MME. L'HEUREUX:

> Every time Hélène'd talk about him she'd hang her head and talk in a whisper . . . About the only time I heard Hélène talk in a whisper . . . I think maybe she was the only one that ever loved him too . . .

MME. BEAULIEU:

> One day he set his mother's hair on fire and smashed just about everything in the house . . . Well that meant they *had* to put him away.

MME. L'HEUREUX:

> They never gave a damn about that boy while he was at home, but as soon as they put him away, the nut — and she weighed about two hundred pounds in those days — well she started losing weight and Hélène started drinking . . .

MME. GINGRAS:

> And then you should have heard them carrying on . . . Nothing but Claude this and Claude that . . . I never saw the likes of it. They'd go on weepin' and wailin' for days at a stretch . . .

MME. TREMBLAY:

> Claude in the sanatorium, now there was a real tragedy for them, a real grand tragedy in their lives. So now they could do anything in the name of the family tragedy!

MME. L'HEUREUX:

> Claude is thirty-five years old now. Fifteen years they've had him locked up . . . He'll never get outa the hatch now . . .

MME. BERNIER:
>When I was a kid I used to play with him once in a
>while . . . Not very often though . . . I don't know
>why, he was always talking about Québec City . . .
>Always used to say how he wanted to get to Québec
>City. That's why sometimes when he wanted to play
>with the rest of us we'd all yell, "Go on, pigeon, go
>to Québec City! Québec City's that away, pigeon! . . ."
>They used to call him pigeon because he had such a
>pigeon brain . . .

ALL THE WOMEN:
>Pigeon! . . . Pigeon! . . . Pigeon! . . .

>*ROBERTINE is at her window. She has let the
>shade up.*

ROBERTINE:
>Hélène is asleep. She finally got herself calmed down
>. . . It's so nice out . . . I would have liked to've been
>able to come out and sit on the porch myself . . . But
>no, I don't even have the right to that much! To tell
>the truth, I've never had the right to much of anything,
>when it comes right down to it . . .

>*Silence.*

>Nothing! Not a damn thing! I never had nothing!

>*Silence.*

>Nothin'. I was born in this house, I was brought up
>in this house, I got married in this house . . . I had
>my kids . . . I wouldn't be surprised if they buried
>the damn house along with me . . . I had ignorant
>parents, a bastard of a husband . . . And kids that
>aren't normal . . . But I kept up the fight though!
>I'm not a quitter, not me, I did what I could. Not
>that there was all that much I could do, I suppose.
>I raised 'em the best way I knew how, those kids

of mine . . . It's not my fault if . . . No, it's not my
fault . . . I put up with their father as long as I could,
I put up with Henri as long as I could, but now . . .
Now I've had it, I just can't put up with anything anymore. It won't be long . . . It won't be long now, it'll
all be over, I won't have to worry about nothing . . .
Be good to your children, give them everything you've
got, and they'll curse you for it as long as they live!
And you'll end up your days all alone, shoved away
in a corner, like a beggar in your own house.

Long silence.

She smiles.

When Hélène and Claude were little, I'd come out and
sit on the porch in the evening. Hélène, she'd be
down playing with Carmen and Rose, and Claude,
he'd sit up here beside his mother. He'd just sit there
quiet beside me, and I'd talk away to him about this
and that . . . I don't know if he always understood,
but he'd sit there and listen just the same. And then
when I'd stop talking, he'd ask me to go on and . . .
Well . . . I'd go on.

Very long silence.

It's better than nothing, I guess.

*The women, one by one, disappear from their
windows.*

seven

Nighttime.

CLAUDE enters very quietly into the empty courtyard. He looks all around, smiling. He goes to Robertine's window, and tries to see into the house. He sits down on the porch steps with the waddling motions of a little boy, then gets up and goes into the house.

CLAUDE:

They didn't even get the house ready! They didn't even take out the furniture.

He laughs.

They didn't even get the house ready. I knew it! They didn't want me to come. They never want me to come. But I came anyway. I bet they won't even recognize me with my sunglasses on.

He laughs.

CLAUDE:

> Maybe they won't be able to see me. Yeah, they'll
> come home, they'll come in and they won't be able
> to see me! It'll be just like I wasn't there. Like when
> I was little. And they'll talk and say stuff like I wasn't
> there and then if they notice I'm there they'll say,
> "It doesn't matter, he can't understand, he's too
> young." Either that or else they'll talk in English.
> But they can't fool me 'cause I'm gonna play a dirty
> trick on them. I put on my sunglasses to make me
> invisible and I learned how to talk English!

> *ROBERTINE appears in the living room door-*
> *way.*

ROBERTINE:

> Claude!

> *He turns around sharply.*

CLAUDE:

> It's her again! She can always see me, that one!
> You're not wearing white! I told you, you're supposed
> to wear white!

ROBERTINE:

> Claude, what are you doing here?

CLAUDE:

> You're not wearing white!

ROBERTINE:

> Did you come with the brother? Did the brother
> bring you here, Claude?

CLAUDE:

> You're not wearing white! You're doing that on
> purpose, aren't you! . . . You always do the opposite
> of what I ask you to . . . Everything's gotta be white,
> Mom! Everything!

> *FRANCINE comes in as well.*

ROBERTINE:
    Claude, answer me!

CLAUDE:
    You're not wearing white, you either, Francine!
    Don't you ever listen to me? What are you doing
    here anyway? I wasn't expecting you! Did I ask you
    to come and see me? Are you coming to yell at me
    again?

        ROBERTINE goes a bit closer.

    Don't you come any closer, my powers'll make you
    drop dead. Did Hélène come with you too? Did she
    put on her fancy white dress with the plunging
    neckline? Not her either, eh? You dress up all
    coloured when you come to see me. I told you to
    dress in white when you come here!

ROBERTINE: *still coming closer*
    Claude! . . . Claude! . . . You're not in the hospital
    here . . . You're at home . . . How did you get home,
    Claude. And take off those sunglasses, there, they
    don't look very nice . . .

CLAUDE:
    What sunglasses?

        He touches his glasses, looks around.

    You're not supposed to see me when I've got my
    sunglasses on. Not even you! And you're supposed
    to talk English. You'll see! I'll understand everything
    you say! At the hospital, when I've got my sunglasses
    on I disappear into the walls and they can talk English
    all they like, I understand every word! Everything!
    I can do that because of my powers!

ROBERTINE:
    Don't talk so loud. Hélène and Henri are still sleeping . . .

CLAUDE:
>I can do all kinds of things with my powers, Mom.
>I can make stuff appear and disappear and everything!
>
>*His expression suddenly changes.*
>
>Only sometimes they don't disappear. Sometimes
>they don't disappear, they just stay there, Mom, and
>I get scared.
>
>*ROBERTINE comes right up to CLAUDE. She
>takes him by the shoulders.*

ROBERTINE:
>Claude, look at me. Look at me, like a good boy.
>
>*She gently takes off his sunglasses.*
>
>The same eyes as last time . . . If you've run away,
>Claude, I won't scold you. I promise, I won't scold
>you at all.

CLAUDE:
>I didn't run away! It was them that sent me away!
>They didn't want me any more. They didn't want
>me there anymore, Mom! They said I hurt somebody
>but it was just 'cause I was defending myself. I only
>hit him because he was trying to poison me, Mom!

ROBERTINE:
>Francine, look and see if there's a car outside.

CLAUDE:
>There's no car. D'you think they'd go and drive me
>back? No sir! I had to thumb!

FRANCINE:
>Maybe you'd better phone the hospital, Grandma.

CLAUDE:

> No! Don't phone the hospital! Don't phone the hospital, they'll come and get me!

ROBERTINE:

> So that's it! . . . You did run away . . .

CLAUDE:

> And you didn't even get the house ready! After I went and learned English and everything!

FRANCINE: *to ROBERTINE*

> Go phone them, I'll stay here with him.

ROBERTINE:

> Are you crazy? He's liable to turn on you!

FRANCINE:

> No, he's not. You know very well he's always nice to me . . . He's gentle as a lamb . . .

ROBERTINE:

> Well watch out . . . I won't be long . . . I'll tell them to send an ambulance . . . Just make sure Hélène doesn't wake up and find him here, that's all . . .

> *She exits.*

CLAUDE:

> She's scared, eh, Francine? She's scared of me. They're all scared of me. You know, when I take my sunglasses off, and I appear again, I grow, zoom, just like that! Don't you ever grow? You're not afraid, are you? It's alright, I haven't got my sunglasses anymore . . . I'm dangerous without my sunglasses! That's right, you can't be afraid of me, you're just a little girl . . .

FRANCINE:

> Yeah, I'm just a little girl. Do you want some peppermints? You like them, don't you . . . ?

She picks up a dish of peppermints off the TV.
During this CLAUDE puts his sunglasses back
on. He looks around, worried.

CLAUDE:

> Hey, little girl, have you got a dime? Can I bum a
> dime off you? I have to phone home . . . My mother's
> sick . . . It's true, my mother's sick! Just a dime.
> You must have one on you.

FRANCINE: *retreating*

> No, I haven't got one.

CLAUDE:

> What do you mean you haven't got one? You did
> just a while ago. I saw you, in the canteen.

FRANCINE: *after a moment of hesitation*

> I spent it all.

CLAUDE:

> Go look in your piggy bank.

FRANCINE:

> I don't have a piggy bank.

CLAUDE:

> Yes, you do. I saw it. Go get a dime out of your
> piggy bank! My mother's sick. And she's coming on
> Sunday. She won't be sick anymore on Sunday and
> she'll come and see me. Give me a dime right now,
> or just you wait, I'll . . .

FRANCINE:

> Well, I'll go look . . . In my room . . .

CLAUDE:

> And hurry up, 'cause if you don't I'm gonna set
> your hair on fire!

FRANCINE exits.

CLAUDE:
> And I'll punch you in the mouth too, you filthy old
> crow! Filthy old crow! You're nothing but a filthy
> old crow, Brother Handy-Hands!

ROBERTINE re-enters

ROBERTINE: *very softly*
> Claude, that's no way to talk. Don't talk like that,
> Claude . . . I just spoke to the brother . . . He said
> he's given you a nice holiday . . .

CLAUDE:
> He's a dirty liar! Because I grew here! He wouldn't
> give me a dime to phone, so I jumped on him.

He starts to laugh.

> And then I grew here! He didn't think I could, eh,
> well I put on my sunglasses, and I disappeared!

HELENE:
> Let me past! I want to see him!

FRANCINE:
> No, don't! He doesn't look very good.

HELENE:
> Let me past!

HELENE enters, almost running.

CLAUDE:
> Get out of here, you! Don't come any closer! It was
> you that sent me here! Mom, tell her to get out of
> here! I don't want to see her! She's the one that
> turned me in here! You're the one, you old bitch!
> You drove me out here, and you wouldn't even let
> me carry my own suitcase . . .

HELENE:
> Claude, listen to me . . .

CLAUDE:
> Get out!

ROBERTINE:
> Hélène, get out! There's nothing you can do here.
> Leave it to me . . . I'm trying to humour him . . .

> *HELENE exits. CLAUDE goes up to*
> *ROBERTINE, very slowly.*

CLAUDE: *as if holding a phone receiver*
> It's a long time since you've been to visit me, Mom . . .

ROBERTINE: *not catching on right away*
> I just haven't been able to lately, Claude . . .

CLAUDE:
> Why don't you come to see me, Mom? I'm all alone
> here. And they want to kill me. They want to poison
> me, Mom! They put poison in everything. Why
> don't you come and see me, Mom? I'm lonesome.
> I'm all by myself here. Won't you come and see me
> next Sunday?

ROBERTINE:
> I can't Claude. I'm sick . . .

CLAUDE:
> Are you sick? Is it because of Hélène? Is Hélène
> making you sick? Tell me and I'll hit her for you.
> Is it her, Mom?

ROBERTINE:
> No, Claude, it's not her. It's just that I'm not well . . .

CLAUDE:
> The brother gave me a dime to phone you, Mom.
> That was nice of him, wasn't it?

> *ROBERTINE realizes he thinks he's on the*
> *phone.*

ROBERTINE:

>Yes, that was nice of him . . .

CLAUDE:

>Wasn't that nice of him? He gave me a dime and said, "Go phone your mother, Claude, and tell her you can go home now . . ." Are you glad I phoned?

>>*He motions to her to talk on the phone, like him. She pretends to pick up a receiver.*

ROBERTINE:

>Yes. Yes, Claude, I'm very glad . . .

CLAUDE:

>Hey, Mom, you've got to come and get me right away. My suitcase is all ready. You've got to come right away! Right now! They want to kill me!

ROBERTINE:

>No, no, Claude! No, they don't. Don't think like that!

CLAUDE:

>Yes, they want to kill me! They've got it all planned. Can you hear me, Mom?

ROBERTINE:

>Yes, I can hear you.

CLAUDE:

>I can't talk any louder. I'm hiding from them to phone you. The brother didn't want to give me the money so I asked the little girl from downstairs . . . I'm so glad to talk to you, Mom . . .

ROBERTINE:

>I'm glad to talk to you too, Claude . . .

>>*Long silence.*

ROBERTINE:
Did you get the sweater I sent you? Does it fit alright?
Is it warm enough?

Long silence.

She smiles.

Are you eating alright? Are you eating alright, Claude?

CLAUDE: *speaking gradually more quietly*
No, I'm eating less and less . . . They say I'm getting
fat, but it isn't true. You should see me, Mom. You
should see me. I'm sick, and I want to come home!

ROBERTINE:
You can't come home right away, Claude. The
brother said to wait a bit longer . . . You're not well
enough . . . You hang up now . . . Are you going to
hang up for Mother?

CLAUDE:
No, I want to talk to you some more. Just a bit
longer, Mom. Just a bit. Are you going to come on
Sunday?

ROBERTINE:
I don't know, dear . . .

CLAUDE:
Are you going to come on Sunday, Mom? The brother
said you were going to come.

ROBERTINE:
That's right, I'll try to come on Sunday, Claude . . .

CLAUDE:
Do you promise?

ROBERTINE:
Yes, yes, I promise, but you hang up now.

She yells very loud, almost in desperation.

ROBERTINE:

Hang up, Claude, Mother just can't talk to you any more!

HELENE appears in the doorway. She has changed into a white dress.

HELENE:

Are you out of your mind or what? What kind of a way is that to talk to him?!

CLAUDE:

They're not coming!

HELENE:

If you go on talking to him like that you're only going to make things worse!

ROBERTINE:

Look, you stay out of this! It's none of your business! After the scene you made before you went to bed you oughta be ashamed of yourself! I suppose now you're sober again all of a sudden, eh? Have you forgotten everything? Now you're going to be nice and I'm not allowed to say anything, is that it? Get out of here and leave this to me. I'm used to him!

HELENE:

Acting like a lunatic, is that your idea of being used to him?

CLAUDE:

Well, if they don't come, then I'm going myself, anyway!

HELENE:

I put on the dress I wore the last time we went to see him . . . I thought that might quiet him down . . . Go put on your white dress too. Francine's putting her's on.

95

*ROBERTINE looks at HELENE and CLAUDE
for a long time, then slowly exits.*

ROBERTINE:
Alright . . . I'll go put on my white dress . . .

*HELENE goes up to CLAUDE who is hiding in
a corner.*

HELENE:
Well now, how's my little brother, how are you doing?
Long time no see, eh?

*CLAUDE turns away quickly, but when he sees
HELENE's white dress he smiles.*

CLAUDE:
It's you! I wasn't expecting you.

HELENE:
Now, now, did you think we'd forgotten you?

CLAUDE:
Where are they, the rest of them?

HELENE:
They're coming . . . They're coming. We've been
getting all ready to come see you for a couple of
days now. You see, I wore my white dress . . .

CLAUDE:
Yes. I'm glad . . . All white . . . You're pretty . . .
Mom too?

HELENE:
Yes. And Francine too. And Henri too.

CLAUDE:
Henri's coming? This is the first time he's come.
He never wanted to come before. I'm glad.

HELENE puts her hand to her forehead.
She is close to tears.

HELENE:

> Hey . . . Why don't we sit down, eh? . . . Do you want
> to? . . . We'll have a little chat . . .

They sit down.

Embarrassed silence.

CLAUDE stands up and goes to get the dish of
peppermints on the TV set. He offers them to
HELENE. She takes one. When he sees that
HELENE has put the peppermint in her mouth
and that it's not poisoned, he takes a handful
and stuffs them all into his mouth.

HELENE:

> So, how have you been?

CLAUDE: *chewing*

> Oh, fine. Everything's always been fine . . . You
> know that! Oh, Hélène, you don't know how crazy
> they are! If you knew what they're trying to do to
> me!

He looks around.

> I know he's watching me . . .

HELENE:

> Who?

CLAUDE:

> That filthy old Brother Handy-Hands! He's always
> watching me! He won't let go of me! He doesn't
> want me to phone you. I think he wants me to stay
> here all the time. He gives me stuff to drink, Hélène!
> He's trying to poison me!

HELENE:

> No, no, Claude, you know nobody's trying to poison you . . .

CLAUDE:

> Yes they are! I know they're trying to poison me! I know everything that goes on around here. But one of these days I'm gonna get them all with my powers! I'll get 'm all! The whole bunch o' them! Just you wait, Hélène, I'll blow them all up good, you'll see!

> *He takes more peppermints.*

> How come the rest of them aren't here yet?

HELENE:

> They won't be long . . . You know, since Henri started limping . . .

CLAUDE:

> Henri limps now?

> *Silence.*

HELENE: *to herself*

> Yeah . . . Yeah, he limps alright!

CLAUDE:

> Then he doesn't walk around with his sandwich outfit on any more?

HELENE:

> Huh?

CLAUDE:

> Yeah, when I was home, the last time, he used to walk around the streets, dressed like a sandwich man . . .

HELENE:

Ah! God, that was ages ago, that . . . Uh . . . No,
he's not a sandwich man any more . . . He didn't do
that for very long . . .

CLAUDE:

That's too bad. He looked so funny . . . I told everybody here that my brother-in-law walks around dressed
like a sandwich . . . They all thought that was real
funny . . . The brother, he said I was only saying that
because all I ever think about is food, but it's not true!
I don't eat anything anymore! And pretty soon . . .
I'm gonna shrink and get teeny, teeny, teeny . . .
And then I'll disappear . . . I won't need my sunglasses
anymore . . . And I'll kill them all! And then I'll
come home and sit on the back porch.

Silence.

Did you come to get me, Hélène? You always say in
your letters that you're going to come and get me.
That's why you're dressed in white, because you've
come to get me, eh?

HELENE takes CLAUDE in her arms.

HELENE:

Yes, Claude, I've come to get you.

Silence.

Claude . . . Claude, do you know where you are?

CLAUDE:

Sure, here, in the hospital! It's because I'm sick.
The brother says my head doesn't . . . Doesn't work
too good.

HELENE:

> I'm going to take you back home, Claude, and then
> you'll see, your head'll get better. You'll be able to
> rest up, and then we'll find some work for you to
> do . . . Something that isn't too tiring . . .

CLAUDE:

> Are you still working on the Main?

HELENE:

> No, I've been working in a little cafe on Papineau
> Street for the last few months. But it's just for the
> time being. Maurice is going to take me back on in
> his nightclub. If you want, you can come and work
> with me.

CLAUDE:

> No, never!

HENRI:

> I tell you I'm not going in there!

FRANCINE:

> Yes, you are, Daddy!

HENRI:

> I look like some kind of nut in this get-up!

CLAUDE:

> I don't wanna go back to that club! They were the
> ones, Toothpick and them, who started putting
> things in my drinks, Hélène . . . They put powder in
> my drinks, don't you remember? And they thought
> it was so funny because it made me see things . . .

HELENE:

> He still remembers that . . . No, no Claude, you know
> they didn't do that . . . Don't think about that
> anymore . . . They never did anything like that.

CLAUDE: *stands up suddenly*
Yes, I remember! I remember what it did to me,
Hélène!

*He sees HENRI and FRANCINE dressed in
white.*

He freezes for a few seconds.

Here they are! Here they are!

*He goes over to HENRI who is obviously
very scared.*

Henri! It's been so long . . . You're walking with a
cane now? Are you sick too?

HENRI:
Yes.

FRANCINE:
Here's your dime, Uncle Claude.

CLAUDE:
What do you want me to do with that? The brother
gives me dimes when I want to phone! Where's Mom?

HENRI:
She's coming.

CLAUDE:
Well, come and sit down and wait for her . . .

They all sit down.

Embarrassed silence.

He passes the peppermints.

They're alright, they're good . . .

He sits back down again.

HELENE:
Francine's started at a new school . . .

HELENE motions her to say say something.

FRANCINE:
Yes . . . I'm going to be a hairdresser . . .

CLAUDE:
A hairdresser? To give people hairdos?

He starts to laugh.

But you're too young . . .

FRANCINE:
No, I'm not . . . I'm almost sixteen . . .

*ROBERTINE appears, also dressed in white.
CLAUDE doesn't see her. She sits to one side.*

CLAUDE:
No, you can't fool me. Sixteen!? You're just a little
girl. Henri, she's not sixteen, is she?

*HENRI doesn't answer. He buries himself
behind a newspaper.*

FRANCINE:
Yes, I am, Uncle. I'm fifteen, I'll be sixteen in two
months . . . I'm almost grown up! It's just that you
haven't seen me for a long time.

CLAUDE:
No, you're being silly! Hey, Hélène? Francine's
only ten, isn't she?

HELENE:
Yes. She's only ten.

HENRI moves to turn on the TV.

HELENE.
     Henri!

HENRI:
     Well, what am I supposed to say to him? You expect
     me to talk to him? What am I supposed to say to
     him? He's crazy!

CLAUDE:
     Crazy? Who? Who's crazy? Me? So you think I'm
     crazy too, eh? You bastard, I'm gonna kill you! And
     you won't be the first one either! You want to poison
     me and make me look crazy, Toothpick!

ROBERTINE:
     Claude!

     CLAUDE turns sharply towards his mother.

CLAUDE:
     Mom! You're wearing white!

     *He rushes to sit at the feet of ROBERTINE,
     and lays his head on her knees.*

     You've come to get me, Mom! All dressed in white!
     You look just like a Holy Virgin!

ROBERTINE:
     A Holy Virgin . . .

HENRI: *to Hélène*
     Go phone the police! Do something! We'll all get
     our throats cut!

FRANCINE:
     Shut up! You're as crazy as he is!

ROBERTINE: *running her hand through CLAUDE's hair*
It's been a long time since we've been to see you. But
it's not that we didn't want to . . .

She looks at HELENE, pleadingly.

HELENE:
No, it's not that we didn't want to . . . It's because
Mother hasn't been well . . . That's why . . .

Silence.

ROBERTINE:
Have you made any friends since the last time? Do
you talk to the others a bit? Tell Mother what you
do all day . . .

CLAUDE:
Every morning the bells wake me up. Boy, do they
ever ring! Those bells, they ring so loud . . . And
long . . . Dong! . . . Dong! . . . It doesn't do any good
to tell them I've already heard them, they keep ringing
anyway! Then, I get up right away, put my sunglasses
on and I go straight to the window. And all day in the
park the cowboys and Indians play bows and arrows.
All day long, Mom. I'm lucky they can't see me 'cause
I've got my sunglasses on. Then when the brother
comes to call me for lunch I say no, and I run away.
Sometimes I'm so scared of the poison they put in
my food I run right out of the hospital into the
middle of the bows and arrows. When I get in there
I take off my sunglasses. Then the cowboys and
Indians can see me! I'd rather get shot by an arrow
than get poisoned, Mom. Can't you say anything?

ROBERTINE:
I'm listening, Claude. I'm listening. But you've got
to understand nobody's trying to poison you.

CLAUDE:

Yes, they are. They are, I know it. There's nothing I can do about it, Mom! There's nothing I can do about it, they're gonna get me if it keeps up!

ROBERTINE:

There's nothing I can do about it either, Claude. If you keep talking like that I'm going to call the brother. I was talking to him, just a while ago, and he wasn't too happy with you.

CLAUDE, worried, stands up and goes back to sit near HELENE.

CLAUDE:

Your legs really hurt, Henri?

HENRI:

Yup, they really hurt.

CLAUDE:

Ah . . .

Smiling.

Then I'm not the only sick one after all . . . You're staying a long time!

The rest look at each other.

FRANCINE:

Well, didn't you want us to come?

CLAUDE:

No.

He puts his sunglasses back on.

I wanted to come and see you . . .

ROBERTINE:
>   Claude, listen to me. I've called a taxi . . . It'll be
>   here any minute now. We've come to get you,
>   Claude.

CLAUDE:
>   Is that right? The brother says I can go!

ROBERTINE:
>   Yes.

CLAUDE:
>   And my suitcase?

ROBERTINE:
>   You won't need one.

>   *She rubs her hand across her forehead.*

>   We'll . . . We'll get you all new clothes . . .

CLAUDE:
>   White?

ROBERTINE:
>   Yes, white.

>   *ROBERTINE stands up and goes to wave at
>   window.*

CLAUDE: *to FRANCINE*
>   We're going home, Francine! We're going home!
>   I can't wait! I can't wait!

>   *The doorbell rings.*

>   It's him! It's the taxi!

ROBERTINE:
>   Yes. Come on, Claude . . . Come here, Hélène, I'll
>   need you . . .

CLAUDE:
> Hey, I'm going home! Did you empty out the house?
> Did you paint the house all white? I don't want to
> see the old furniture you know . . .

ROBERTINE:
> Yes, we've done all that . . .

CLAUDE:
> Is it all, all empty?

HELENE:
> Yes.

FRANCINE:
> Come on, Daddy . . .

HENRI:
> No.

> *He remains seated.*

> *HELENE, ROBERTINE and FRANCINE
> surround CLAUDE.*

> *The doorbell rings again.*

> *ROBERTINE takes CLAUDE's head in her
> hands. She looks in his eyes.*

ROBERTINE:
> Forgive me, Claude! For everything!

> *The characters stay motionless for a few
> seconds. Then, slowly, HENRI lowers his
> newspaper.*

HENRI:
> There's not a goddam thing I can do! I can't even
> go out of the house any more. I'm stuck in here
> with this cane. Goddam cane! They won't let me

go outside because they're ashamed of me. Well I'm ashamed of them too. Ok, so I've never been awfully bright, I know, but them . . . Hélène is smart, she was always at the head of the class in school and everything . . . But that don't stop her being crazy as a loon just the same.

>*He laughs.*

HENRI:
>To think she ran after me for two years to get me to marry her . . . She's gotta be off her rocker! Claude's about the only one, when you come right down to it . . . Claude, at least with him you know he's a nut for real. They didn't have to drive him crazy, he's crazy already. He's better off than any of us!

HENRI & HELENE:
>There's not a goddam thing I can do . . .

>>*From this point on we hear all the neighbours murmuring, "There's not a goddam thing I can do" until the end.*

HELENE:
>Boy, am I ever scrapin' the barrel working in this dump! Me, a club waitress, winding up in a smoke meat joint on Papineau! Not much farther down you can go, is there? Well, yes, I guess there is . . . And I've been there! What I did last night, that was the real bottom of the bucket, that was! I got plastered because I figured I could get myself arrested. Like last time! But they didn't even stop me . . . And yet the judge said last time, once more and he'd throw me in the jug. Last night I wanted to go to jail. I'd rather get hauled down to the Number 4 than have to go back to that place! I can't stand the sight of them any more! Sometimes I could just kill Henri, squash him like a bug, just to get myself arrested! I never go through with it though. I don't feel like swinging at the end of any rope! . . . Now prison,

I wouldn't care, you get your room and board, and
you meet some new faces . . . But not the end of a
rope, no thanks . . .

She looks at HENRI.

HELENE:
> He ain't worth it . . . Only one of these days I'll end
> up doing it . . . I know some day I'm gonna do it . . .
> And then again . . . Huh . . . I doubt it . . .

HELENE, HENRI
& FRANCINE:
> There's not a goddam thing I can do . . .

FRANCINE:
> I'll never even make it as a hairdresser. My nerves
> are too bad. My nerves were too bad for me to go on
> any farther in school so they told me I should learn
> a trade . . . But there's nothing I can do. It's no use.
> I'm not good enough to be a hairdresser. I can't
> work with my hands. My mind's always off on
> something else when I work. I can never concentrate
> on what I'm doing. Something in my head clicks off
> everytime I try . . . If only I was smart like Mom,
> I could try to do something. But no, I have to take
> after the old man . . .

HENRI, HELENE, FRANCINE
& ROBERTINE:
> There's not a goddam thing I can do . . .

ROBERTINE:
> Be good to your children, knock yourself out to give
> them everything and they'll hate you for it the rest
> of their lives. Then you'll end up your days all alone,
> shoved in a corner, like a beggar in your own house.

ALL:
>
> There's not a goddam thing I can do!

CLAUDE:
>
> I can do anything, I can! I've got all the powers!
> That's because of my sunglasses. I'm the only one . . .
> The only one that's got sunglasses!

TALONBOOKS — PLAYS IN PRINT 1975

Colours in the Dark — James Reaney
The Ecstasy of Rita Joe — George Ryga
Captives of the Faceless Drummer — George Ryga
Crabdance — Beverley Simons
Listen to the Wind — James Reaney
Esker Mike & His Wife, Agiluk — Herschel Hardin
Sunrise on Sarah — George Ryga
Walsh — Sharon Pollock
Apple Butter & Other Plays for Children — James Reaney
The Factory Lab Anthology — Connie Brissenden, ed.
The Trial of Jean-Baptiste M. — Robert Gurik
Battering Ram — David Freeman
Hosanna — Michel Tremblay
Les Belles Soeurs — Michel Tremblay
API 2967 — Robert Gurik
You're Gonna Be Alright Jamie Boy — David Freeman
Bethune — Rod Langley
Preparing — Beverley Simons
Forever Yours, Marie-Lou — Michel Tremblay
En Pièces Détachées — Michel Tremblay
Three Plays by Eric Nicol — Eric Nicol
Lulu Street — Ann Henry
Bonjour la Bonjour — Michel Tremblay
Some Angry Summer Songs — John Herbert
Fifteen Miles of Broken Glass — Tom Hendry
Jacob's Wake — Michael Cook